Tempest

Wild Weather Collections

Edited by Sam Bellamy
Green Ink Poetry Press

Tempest

Foreword

Our second Wild Weather collection called for beautiful works exploring *Tempest*; sea storms, the power of nature, relationships, and how our environment can change us are all themes touched upon in this collection.

The result is a stunning range of interpretations from thirty-five incredibly talented contributors, exploring the themes in ways we could not have expected, as well as works that fit our ideal for Tempest perfectly. We hope that you enjoy reading all of the work here as much as we did!

All of our contributors are also featured on our website – https://www.greeninkpoetry.co.uk/ - where you can find their biographies and links to their other work.

Contents

Contents cont.

Nature's Furies
Felicity Conneely

Ominous figures race

across the darkening sky.

In the distance,

galahs shriek seeking shelter

before the heavens

unburden themselves.

Anxious eyes scan

the remote horizon

trying to predict

the next calamity.

Countless seafarers have borne witness,

victims of an unmerciful force.

Swept ashore on foreign isles,

from centuries long before.

For there is no foolproof

means of prediction,

no divination,

no soothsayer's prophecy.

Instead, only the urge,

buried instinctively within,

to hold on tight

as nature's furies

sweep away all that is.

storm me sea
Jim Young

in the push and pull of a daring be

in the push and pull of a wild sea

in an all-storm on the bite sea

a seething spit in the face sea

a banshee quivering spume sea

a running running striding sea

life passing before your eyes sea

a claw me back to land sea

in the push and pull of a daring be

Solid Air

Isabel Miles

It started with the crows

having fun with the wind,

slammed back or batted gently to one side,

sent soaring, dropped.

Their aim appeared to be to hold quite still,

balancing the gusts.

Later they disappeared to huddle in the wood,

game over.

The gale had won.

The trees that had been swaying

as in admiration of their aeronautic feats

took centre stage.

Their ballet turned into a maenad's frantic dance,

fantastical and dark with power.

Some touched the ground in rapture or in pain.

Some shattered. Branches, trunks smashed down.

Trees fell in serried lines,

great roots unearthed.

The sea that had been troubled from the start

could find no way to settle,

twitched and squirmed,

threw out untimely blasts of water,

snatched at seagulls struggling for land.

Its waves were an erratic pulse

that flipped whole fleets of fishing boats,

tossed seals ashore.

The ocean's vast heart juddered, shuddered

juddered on.

In all that wind,

earth could not find the space to breathe.

The Storm's Wrath

Helen Openshaw

A clattering, rattling,

Train wreck, car crash of a storm

Hurls its anger over this bloody land.

Each strike is aimed precisely

At the heart of what we know,

And don't know.

A dumb silence rages as lightening

Strikes its target, stealing our

Entitlement, pocketing our sourness.

We blindly rub salt into our wounds,

And turn the other way.

Bonne Tempête

Lauren O'Donovan

Smoke from the village pots rises vertically,

without challenge.

A shield-maiden moves decisively, stirs her foot in a tumult of noise.

Small trees in leaf begin to sway.

    Crested wavelets tumble inland.

        Electricity wires whistle

        above the sea heaping into spindrifts.

        When the ocean wears white,

        ships are lost behind the waves.

            The air is filled with foam and spray.

                Wooden fascia lies on the road.

SW F8 gale expected midnight to 0600

Lesley Curwen

Foam lines horizon-wide on ocean face,
whiteness scrolled on each tremendous wave.
Pinpoints of other light sprig tortured air,
starlets that burn around a compass-rose
impersonate vast trawlers, cardinal buoys,
lighthouse five-miles-off, ship metal-close.

Worse yet, the imperceptible threat of rogue
containers, nomadic storm-scourged trees.
In keening southwesterlies, hours elongate,
our rods and cones straining to apprehend

first greying, night-layers undone, a slow
bleach of edge as blink-flash becomes boat
or quay. Things are reduced to dimensions
we know: we see the hazards in our way.

Troubled Waters
(Haiku Sequence)
Samo Kreutz

heavy tempest
guest at a child's tea party
the lightning bolt

raging water
our castles in the sky
washed away

bluebird on a tree
raised at least a little
storm clouds

Prayer to the Tempest

Elyssa Tappero

Insatiable Charybdis,

drag me like a tiny ship into your chill black waters

shatter my hull, snap my decks, tear away my sails

I offer you my fear; drown it in the deep!

I offer you my hate; drown it in the deep!

I offer you my sorrow; drown it in the deep!

Monstrous Charybdis,

transform what remains of me into teeth and wrath

set my maelstrom heart free to devour the world

I am a vortex too, inside

Weather Warning

Sarah O'Grady

Storm Corrie lifts the keep-net

from our bacchanalian days,

releases all the saggy cans

to dance like cow bells

swung from jowls

tripping down the scree.

Our pastures still

patchy green,

we are half asleep

hearing the end of the world,

dreaming that jetsam

hurled at cars

is surely cattle

clattering in to milk.

The Sea

Peter Burrows

Your stories always come back to that night.

More so now, I hang back – as they go ahead,

To sit with you, to hear talk of what might

Have been. Not your true home these thirty years,

Still yearning for the city of your childhood,

Before marriage, before disappointment.

How can I console for a life lost that meant

Love for you, but none of us being here?

For now, you only see the path you once had.

Now too frail to leave the house. When storms are bad

I think not only of you, but when the sea

Breached defences to your last stand.

You swept it back with the broom. The same sea

That a lifetime ago, scoured lives miles inland.

Shanty Town

Jon Doble

And the fragile little town heard the calling of the storm
as the windows and the doors locked tight,
still, now listening for the music of the night.
Singing..........
down, down, blow the man down.

And the wind sang with gusto preaching to the choir
as the window panes rattle in the rain,
still, now dreading yet the chorus of the pain.
Singing..........
down, down, blow the man down.

And the sea beat the rhythm of the waves upon the sand
with the sticks and the stones of angry words,
still, now choking on the tempo of the chords.
Singing..........
down, down, blow the man down.

And the song of the past still echoes in the ground

as the stories of the deep are handed down,

still, now casting out the lines that always drown.

Singing..........

down, down, blow the man down.

And the songs of the future hope for life beyond the rain

as the legends of the storm shakes the trees,

still, now desperate for the gods to be appeased.

Singing..........

down, down, blow the man down.

The Force of Nature That is Grief
Saroya Whatley

Without warning, without a sign,

It comes for me every time

As massive tidal waves,

A tempest swirling around,

Pulling me into its watery rage,

And I know there is no escape.

Sometimes it's tears

Sometimes it's fear

Sometimes it's nothing

Just the absence of loving,

        Everything.

People. Places. Things.

All one big monsoon

Of apathy.

Nothing to color the grey

Within

Just a world of black and blue

And the in between

Din.

In the whipping wind of its tornado

In the eye of its storm

It's hard to know how time passes

Hard to feel anything but forlorn.

The one thing that ceases to change

That one that continues to stay

Is this chill in my bones

Knowing I'm in its cage.

Is it for my protection?

Or is it for theirs?

Even if I wanted to leave

I don't know if I would dare.

Perhaps that's why I stay

And wait till the turbulence abates

Whenever that may be,

For your absence in my future

Clouds the paths of my fate

And I would like to see clearly.

Brawl

Jessica Taggart Rose

Lashing out all over the place, chaotic, exhilarated, Ciara blows.

Café roof swings perilous, chalked Specials board claps flat, Jet Skis sign twists its neck.

Water, released, flushes gutters, gushes between outer and inner walls, browns seeping ceilings, gags drains.

Dumped on over and over, Thalassa breaches her walls, all swash and fetch.

She squares up at the Harbour Arms; spit and tumult firing upwards, outwards.

Flings seaweed like spaghetti,

turning and

turning. Slams into concrete docks, reels back to clash with herself.

Dual crests peak in conflict, high as gulls. Silvery shrapnel falls, flaring alight.

Blurring, she greens, peaky.

Drags nets through grim and slum.

From the upset barrel of her belly she wrests plastic shards. Pukes chalk, dog fish, dead wood.

Ciara holds back her hair. Thalassa passes out.

Outlook

Jennifer A. McGowan

Shudders in the walls make me queasy.
My husband is asleep. Everything is battened
except me. I slip my feet into workboots,
steal out to the farm buildings. Rain runs
rivers off the shingles. I cup my hands
in the flows, drink deeply.
I don't know why. Soaked, I wander,
stumble, stare out over the Sound where lightning
burns, pink and purple over Race Point Reef.

John and the children will chide me.
But I need to be here, where
the tide is as angry as the sky.

Note: Race Point Reef is at the western end of Fisher's Island, NY

I Want to Sink Ships

Melissa J. Davies

I want to sink ships she says

the words catching beneath her skin

I want to rise up like a storm from the

bottom of the ocean she says

until the seas swirl around me and

the waves reach up rise up leap up

and meet the wind

I want to sink ships she says

the words catch me beneath my skin

The Rage

Sara Ashton

Torn away from the serenity

When you take hold of me.

Overpowered by the ferocity,

You wash over me.

Once delivering me from

Negativity, I was once

Accustomed to the extremities.

The unpredictability

Crashes down and I no longer see.

Skies darkening as the waters

Edge closer.

The storm is on the horizon,

In the air something solemn

Lingers.

Salt Cure II

Beth Hartley

Will you make a place

to sit with me,

where the wild waves

white noise can take me,

and scour me blind.

Pounding all this to nothingness,

so I can stay silent awhile.

But do not let me go.

Do not let me be dragged away.

Keep that hand quite safe in yours

so that I cannot be lost to it,

not completely.

Ground me, remind me

that the sea is not for every day

and rocks must be endured.

Help me keep enough ocean

that I might not forget

it's skill at wearing down

and smoothing

even the darkest night.

Sit with me and keep me, love,

until the storm is passed;

until we simply sit.

Until I dry out,

until the next time.

In the Morning

Sarah Terkaoui

we found the cliff succumbed to the storm,
dropped heavy into the grey broth
of sea below.

Emerging into a spit of rain, the sky
still sulky, we saw the grasses
blown submissive.

A brown underskirt of earth raw, exposed.
Painful looking. The small jawed beach
choked with sludge.

Sand and shell erased, sea froth swallowed
before it could break the shoreline
the wake of waves disappeared.

Foolishly we had thought
the tempest was within us.

Apocalypse

Carola Huttmann

Angry walls of white spume
rise monstrously from the
torrid roiling purple sea;

they hover momentarily above
the waves as if undecided
what to do with their fury.

Then, like a tempestuous toddler
who's forgotten why he's enraged
the foamy mountains of brine

collapse in pathetic displays of
fatigue upon the soothing softness
of the paper brown beach.

The leaden sky above the ocean,
gunmetal grey in its frenzy, empties
its ferocious tears into the depths

below, obliterating all view with its
mists of frustration and distress; an
anger as ancient as time, as old as Earth.

Nature's tempest is the only way it knows
to vent its anger at the God who made Man;
without him the world would be a calmer,

better place, filled with insects, birdsong,
bees and blossoms, trees and grasses
swaying in gentle breezes; fields and fens

where cattle and sheep gently graze;
without Man there would be no wrath,
no desire for vengeance by the sea and sky

no need for rain and wind to wash away
things that spoil the beauty of Planet Earth;
there would be no need for the tears and temper

of sea and sky to show mankind the wrong
it's done; the burden it's given to its children
and children's children; for it is them who will

suffer all the more for what their parents have left
Not for them the glorious tranquility that reigned
when the Planet was first born; only the abject

extremes of flooding, droughts, heat, loss of harvests;
animal life and hunger will signal the onset of the
apocalypse that will bring the world to an end one day

After Grace Darling.

Lucy Atkinson

Ruins,

sing of footsteps on stone

above the water's edge.

I have walked this path before

in dreams, drudging through the sedge grass

and up the wind-splintered

wreckage of a cliffside.

I have watched her,

the lighthouse keeper's daughter,

bone-white in her oilskins,

blizzard tearing at the ribbon on her hat

and remembered how

the fables say that more than driftwood

washes up on these shores.

A hundred times, I've trailed

like a shadow behind a memory

of the day one woman tamed the waves.

Grace, silent in the moonlight

as seas revolt and rise around her.

In daylight, unseeing eyes trace

the distant lines of the Farne islands

but in dreams, her memory remains.

On Leaving Inishbofin Island

Jean Tuomey

Remember-

the wind, how it blew from North beach,

rounded the corner at Middlequarter,

winched open the window,

caught cobwebs from winter,

tossed tangles behind High Island,

the view to the horizon, the sea a blank page

ruled by waves, the week to unfold,

strangers savouring the seascape too,

the lone fisherman leaning over

to raise a lobster pot, Tommy's white geese,

everybody's black and white dogs,

the hens huddled against a stone wall,

the ease of the *green road*,

the scream down the blowhole,

my voice blending with the surge,

gathering myself as I turned back,

warmth from the flat rock in Fawnmore,

and knee high in purple heather – the decision

to return, always return.

.

She Seeks Safe Harbor

Betty Stanton

In the dark space between her broken lips scream out of nothingness, ships looking for shattered lighthouses as the salty darkness rolls in fog full and thick with tears. It is the closest thing to faith she has been able to hold, this callous beach of stones and weeds and laughter landing cold and sharp in spaces where the rocky sand gapes in wide maws, stone teeth gnashing. She seeks safe harbor, finds the salt scalding her skin, finds the memory of a face, frail, licking her wounds.

The Calm Before The Storm

Corinna Board

The sky exhales
the breath that seeds a storm.

Nature braces herself:
the whorl of leaves and birds
subsides, trees creak and dig in their roots.

It's too quiet.

I can hear
my
heart
beating.

Clouds bloom grey;
barely holding in the rain,
the distant drums of thunder
echo across the horizon,
slowly growing louder.

The song of a storm cock peals out
from the yew's steeple,

a sudden breeze rattles the branches
of a two-hundred year old oak,

now it's only a matter of time.

All at Sea

Andy Eycott

It raged that storm,

a black night decade.

Thought folded in on itself

over and over

power in that cresting rage,

hunger in the cavernous bowl.

Mutinous waves thrust and crashed

heaving a guttural scream,

banshee wail of despair.

Mercilessly tossed and buffeted

in those tempestuous waters

that life sometimes exhales.

Somehow a boy survived in that ocean,

in the swell of that dark landless space.

Jackhammer Sea
Erich von Hungen

Jackhammer sea --
table-pounding, overturning,
door-shaking, fist and hand insisting.

Jackhammer, sledgehammer, crowbar --
breaking, breaking, breaking sea, against it --
the resisting globe, the limit, the stop.

Squander, devastator, destroyer.
Anger roaring, pulverizing,
vanishing, just to rise and try again.

Climbing, falling.
Arms like axes -- swinging, swinging.
Knees up, thighs driving, stamping down.
Spending hard, self-destroying,
generation on generation,
wave on wave on wave.

Battling.

Battling the land,

that vessel which contains

and gives you shape.

Rage.

Rage and wind for words.

Rage and wind in place of them.

Rage and so much sand.

Is it only that?

Is the rest, the point of it,

the only thing that's finally broken?

Brother Sea,

I know you, recognize you.

Who of us, though ...,

who will learn it,

our lesson first?

Persephone's Winter

Louise Mather

The shore, ravening for the tide,

trailing the velvet of your myth,

moon poisoned by the blood

of a silver javelin, you unravelled

coils of pearls, stems

sharpened the night

inked from flesh,

I never told you of –

or where would we be

but under the lake,

in the deluged snow

of Persephone's winter –

the mouth of the earth.

The Storm Within
Asma Amjad

The sky fought with the sea,
the day she died.

The unrelenting, everlasting, torrential downpour of hot tears leaving
a chilly trail in their wake.Thunderous screaming, surging through my
veins and the winds. Oh, the winds, harsh winds and loud winds,
crackling winds and sorrowful winds, echoing in my ears and worst of
all: raging storms and violent waves threatening to drown from
within.

And despite it all –
through it all,
I learnt
to swim.

Birthday

Cherry Doyle

My hair is not your colour, eyes are like my father's;
February sea and storm clouds splitting
in the sky above the harbour.
I trace another flare of filigree
around the corners of my eyes.
It's here you seem to shape yourself -
I've found the nicks and thumbprints
in the bathroom mirror, and my hands.

The morning's passed like clouds,
as, elbow cocked across my eyes,
I lie in my pyjamas, refusing to acknowledge
yet another year closing the gap between us.
Perhaps I am avoiding all your salted weather;
shifted into rain and howling at the treetops.
Perhaps what I have been avoiding – lavish dress
and cots and knitted shoes – is just to put a harbour in between us.

It's All I Know

Dominic Weston

Three times the sea

punished the boy

but still he came

In the harbour

she slammed him

onto barnacle studs

grated his side

Do not take me lightly

In the foreshore

she flipped him

headfirst onto seabed

opened his pupil

Do not take me for granted

In the estuary

she lashed him

to outgoing tides

cast him adrift

Do not take me for a fool

Still he returned
unable to help himself
waist deep in her resentment
her waves slapping his face

and he just laughed

I know you!

Changeover

K. S. Moore

When the sea makes snow
it cries in cloud form,
winter is held to its face.

Breath freezes in waves
on a grey underchurn,
day after lightless day.

March offers peace, a raw
brow, but one that might
soften in morning sun.

Let it be spring, this
sea-storm a chance to
fine-tune the patter.

Tears now dew; the sky
unpeeled to a new
exposed cobalt.

Excerpt from 'The Crab'

Andrew C. Kidd

Scrambling over the granite grey slates

it tunnelled itself in search of shelter

under the stone shelves of this rock-pocked place.

Its ten legs could not keep up the pace

with the bombard of watery fury

that trapped it in a narrow crawlway.

The roar of the wave-wall rumbled.

The arterial tide immersed it

so that it jostled to return venous

before being expelled to the sea.

The shelling continued in this bay

to sink the rockpool and all within it.

The waves crashed and crashed until nothing was left

except calm and the sun setting red in the west.

Floodplain
Bex Hainsworth

Skipton, North Yorkshire

The fields are a bowl, filled.
A glacier once scraped out the entrails
of the valley, leaving an oyster shell,
an altar plate ready for silver.

The river bulges
like a dead thing left to the air.
Its mirrored body is burst open:
a hasty gutting. Each pool,
each grey pocket, an amputated scale.
Mallards float on the upturned
belly like pilotfish.

Dry stone walls rise
from the slippery husk, brown and purple,
the exposed veins of a leviathan.

And where the water thickens to mud,
rams stand in the sod, horns curled
into urchins, and observe, unconcerned.

Open gates and fenceposts
gather, shipwrecks in the shallows.
Trees shoulder their broken branches,
masts, crosses, and gesture
in vain towards higher ground.

Wind

Louise Heywood

Can you hear the whispers?
carried on the wind to
tell us secrets of the earth.
Long forgotten, wasted
on the unrelenting mind.
Be *wise*, lest it be our peril.

Into the night of indigo
skies, the *wind* brings on
the change. It can be
a billow or a breeze to
bear the marks of the
witness on land and in sea.

Hear the deep rumbling
growl that makes the
leaves sing the deadly
song of blades. *Watch*
raindrops glisten upon the
window pane to your soul.

Snaking across your face
where the cold wind bites
or the warm wind soothes.
It turns to whip and wash
the webs away. What do
the *whispers* say?

Storm Gone

Pete Chambers

The sea washed the heart out.

Picked the bones clean.

After winter storms, a naked shore.

Van Gogh yellow. Morn dazzle. Radiance of sand.

One Atlantic mile.

The drums of the waves of the ocean sound and

the salt sea wind: pungent, marine,

fractured by the shriek of Oystercatchers, gathers dark cloud.

Storm light fronts,

all rain vine hung,

that trail the horizon. West and West.

Gigantic sea, consoles. Dissolves.

The heart washed out of us. Let it be gone.

I am what's left in the wrack on the strand.

The Ninth Wave

Nora Nadjarian

(after Ivan Ayvazovsky)

The sea was monstrous, Mother. Our bones and hearts heavy
as sacks of salt, we forgot what we looked like, our faces peeled.
Eight waves broke and taught us about judgement. From land
to unknown land, and a savage sky the colour of heat.

I describe it to you because I've drowned in that barbarous sea,
and will never see you again – Will I see you? More than anything,
my tongue is burning with why and why not. Mother, do not ask.

As we rose and fell on the ninth wave I saw Noah in his empty ark,
his body on fire, a torch, a light, a rush, ashes. This history keeps
happening, for centuries. I died tonight. What does it mean?

We didn't take them, the coastguard said, *we didn't let them in
but the sea is all theirs. Let them write a true story, see if they can.*

The End

*A special thank you at the very
end to our Twitter community,
without whom we wouldn't be
here, and to the following journals
for being incredible inspirations:*

Black Bough Poetry
Perhappened
Seaborne Magazine
Fairy Piece Mag
Acropolis Journal
Hedgehog Poetry

Printed in Great Britain
by Amazon

79264300R00047